What Animals Do in Fall

Katie Peters

GRL Consultant Diane Craig,
Certified Literacy Specialist

Lerner Publications ◆ Minneapolis

Lerner Publications
An imprint of Lerner Publishing Group, Inc.
241 First Avenue North
Minneapolis, MN 55401 USA

For reading levels and more information, look up this title at www.lernerbooks.com.

Main body text set in Memphis Pro 24/39
Typeface provided by Linotype.

Photo Acknowledgments
The images in this book are used with the permission of: © GlobalP/iStockphoto, p. 3; © Chase Dekker/Shutterstock Images, pp. 4–5; © suefeldberg/iStockphoto, pp. 6–7, 16 (squirrel); © Firn/iStockphoto, pp. 8–9, 16 (deer); © phototrip/iStockphoto, pp. 10–11; © MichelGuenette/iStockphoto, pp. 12–13; © WestwindPhoto/iStockphoto, pp. 14–15, 16 (bear).

Front Cover: © Katie Davies/iStockphoto

Library of Congress Cataloging-in-Publication Data

Names: Peters, Katie, author.
Title: What animals do in fall / by Katie Peters.
Description: Minneapolis : Lerner Publications, [2024] | Series: Let's look at fall (pull ahead readers - nonfiction) | Includes index. | Audience: Ages 4–7 | Audience: Grades K–1 | Summary: "Emergent readers will discover what animals do to get ready for winter. Full-color photographs and carefully leveled text help readers learn about the world around them. Pairs with the fiction title Beaver Bev"— Provided by publisher.
Identifiers: LCCN 2022033297 (print) | LCCN 2022033298 (ebook) | ISBN 9781728491264 (library binding) | ISBN 9798765603192 (paperback) | ISBN 9781728498188 (ebook)
Subjects: LCSH: Animal behavior—Juvenile literature. | Autumn—Juvenile literature. | Animals—Wintering—Juvenile literature.
Classification: LCC QL753 .P48 2024 (print) | LCC QL753 (ebook) | DDC 591.5—dc23/eng/20220729

LC record available at https://lccn.loc.gov/2022033297
LC ebook record available at https://lccn.loc.gov/2022033298

Manufactured in the United States of America
1 – CG – 7/15/23

Table of Contents

What Animals Do in Fall

In the fall, animals get ready for winter.

Squirrels hide nuts
in the fall.

Deer grow thick fur
in the fall.

Hares grow white fur.
It will match the snow.

Geese fly south. They
go where it is warm.

Bears make dens. They will sleep all winter.

What animals do you see outside in the fall?

Did You See It?

bear

deer

squirrel

Index